THE MOST Disgusting Places ON THE PLANET

BY JOHN PERRITANO

CAPSTONE PRESS

a capstone imprint

Velocity is published by Capstone Press,
1710 Roe Crest Drive, North Mankato, Minnesota 56003.
www.capstonepub.com

Books published by Capstone Press are manufactured with paper
containing at least 10 percent post-consumer waste.

Library of Congress Cataloging-in-Publication Data
Perritano, John.
 The most disgusting places on the planet / by John Perritano.
  p. cm.—(Velocity. Disgusting stuff)
 Includes bibliographical references and index.
 Summary: "Discusses the grossest places in the world, from those people come into
contact with every day such as bathrooms to tourist sites such as Bubble Gum Alley"—
Provided by publisher.
 ISBN 978-1-4296-7533-8 (library binding)
 1. Curiosities and wonders—Juvenile literature. 2. Aversion—Miscellanea—Juvenile
literature. 3. Hazardous geographic environments—Juvenile literature. I. Title.
AG243.P37 2012
031.02—dc23   2011029182

Editor: Barbara Linde
Project Manager: Archna Bisht
Art Director: Suzan Kadribasic
Designers: Ankita Sharma, Isha Khanna, Manish Kumar
Image Researcher: Ranjana Batra

Photo Credits
Alamy: Stephen Power 6-7, Adrian Arbib, 12-13; AP Images: Matt Slocum, 42-43, Rusty Kennedy,
44-45; Dreamstime: Sergey Zavalnyuk, 4-5, Sebastian Kaulitzki, 8 (bottom); Fotolia: Steve Mann, 34-
35; Getty Images: Jordan Siemens/The Image Bank, 40, Todd Bigelow/Aurora, 40-41; iStockphoto:
Henrik Jonsson Graphic Design, 7, Michael Pettigrew, 11, Chris Fertnig, 28, Bart Coenders, 30-31;
Photolibrary: Simon Fraser/Science Photo Library, Cover, PhotoStock-Israel/Age fotostock, title,
16-17, Michael Siluk, 8-9, Photolibrary, 10-11, 36–37, S.J. Krasemann/Peter Arnold Images, 22-23,
CNS/Sinopictures, 25, Fotoe/Sinopictures, 26-27, Frank Deschandol & Philippe Sabine, 26, Peter
Menzel/Science Photo Library, 28-29, Michael Donne, 35, Eric Brown/Age fotostock, 38-39; Reuters:
Dadang Tri, 24-25; Science Photo Library: Edward Kinsman, 38-39; Shutterstock: Baltik, 8, Smith &
Smith, 14-15, Kirsanov, 20, Dmitry Zamorin , 20-21, Alex Kuzovlev, 26-27, Tyler Olson, 30, Mikus,
Jo., 32-33, Oleg Kozlov, 38; State University of New York at Buffalo, 21; Thinkstock: Photodisc/
Valueline, 14-15, Jupiterimages/Photos.com, 15, Hemera, 18-19

Printed in the United States of America in Stevens Point, Wisconsin.
102011   006404WZS12

Table of Contents

THAT'S SO Disgusting!

Did you ever use your foot to flush a dirty toilet? Do you hold your breath when passing by the garbage dump? Have you turned on the lights only to see cockroaches run away?

Earth is full of beautiful things. But Earth can be pretty disgusting too!

There's a river in Indonesia that's so full of garbage that no fish or plants can live in it. Nearly 20 million bats live in a cave in Texas. All 20 million of them poop on the cave floor. A lake in China is so poisonous that its water will peel your skin if you touch it.

Many places are disgusting. Some are closer than you think. So, put on some old clothes, hold your nose, and turn the page. Let's visit some of the most revolting places in the world. You might be surprised at what you find!

Chapter 1

HORRIBLE HOMES

There's no place like home! But who knows what creatures lurk under the floorboards, in your bed, or on the kitchen floor. Your house could be one of the most disgusting places around.

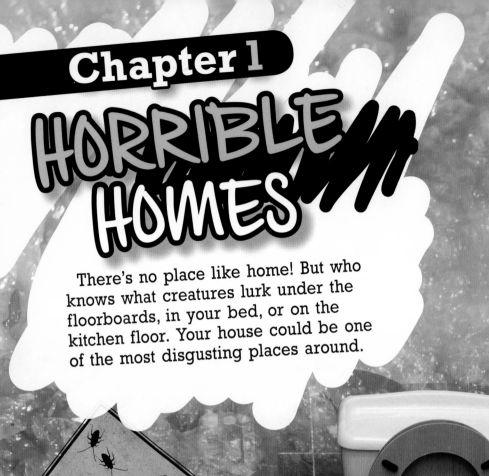

FACT

The average person will spend more than a year in the bathroom during his or her lifetime.

Abominable
Bathrooms

Have you ever wondered what comes between you and the toilet seat? A lot of things.

Bathrooms are gross. Faucet handles are filthy. Toilets are germ factories. The water in the toilet is brimming with **bacteria** from poop. These bacteria can make you sick. Flushing a toilet releases a spray of water. The mist carries germs into the air. The germs land on the floor, in the sink, and on bath towels and wash cloths, polluting everything they touch. Closing the toilet lid before flushing helps, but bacteria can sneak through the gap between the rim and seat.

Your toothbrush is another germ carrier. Germs from your mouth stick to the bristles. And if that's not bad enough, germs from the toothbrush sitting next to yours can jump onto your brush!

But don't fret. Doctors say it's hard for bathroom germs to make you sick. You'll probably be OK as long as your **immune system** is healthy.

bacteria under a microscope

bacteria—very small living things that exist all around you and inside you; some bacteria cause disease
immune system—the part of the body that protects against germs and diseases

Cruddy
Kitchens

Would you believe that your kitchen might be dirtier than your bathroom?

People use sponges and towels to clean their counters. Sponges soak up germs from uncooked meat and chicken. People then use the same germ-filled sponges to clean other things in the kitchen. People may think they are cleaning, but they are actually spreading the germs around!

Sponges and dish towels aren't the only germy spots in the kitchen. Faucet handles, refrigerator door handles, and doorknobs are crawling with bacteria. Why? Because those are places people touch with their hands. If people don't have clean hands, the germs jump onto all sorts of things.

bacteria under a microscope

FACT

Two out of every 10 coffee cups in your cabinet may be covered with bacteria. That's because the sponge you used to clean them was likely filled with germs.

Beastly
Basements

Some people are afraid of basements. And it's no wonder. Many basements are creepy, dark, and **musty**.

Mold is a type of fungus. Many basements contain mold because mold thrives in dark and damp places. Most basements are damp because they are built below ground. In the summer when **humidity** is high, the basement becomes even more damp.

Mold grows on wood, paper, and carpet. In nature, most fungi help the environment. But mold is the last thing you want in your house. Mold moves through the air as tiny **spores**. They can make it hard for some people to breathe. Mold can make a person's nose run. It can also make people sneeze.

Rodents love basements too. Sometimes rats and mice hide in basements. They can eat through many things, including walls. And where they eat, they also poop.

musty—smelly, old, or damp

humidity—the measure of the moisture in the air

spore—a plant cell that develops into a new plant

termites

Cellar Dwellers

Insects and other pests love basements. They crawl in through small holes. Silverfish, termites, centipedes, carpenter ants, and spiders can make a basement a house of horrors. These critters make nests in basements. They lay eggs and spin webs. Some insects chew wooden stairs and beams.

House of Poop

You've heard of a house of cards?
In Kenya you might see a house of poop!

In Kenya and some other nations in Africa, the Maasai
people live as they always have. Their way of life depends
on the cows they herd. The Maasai drink cow milk. They
drink cow blood. They also use cow **dung** to build
their homes!

When Maasai women build homes, they use sticks and
grass. Then they mix mud and cow dung to hold the branches
together. Finally, they build walls with the poopy mixture.

The women then spread cow dung on the outside walls.
This process keeps the huts warm in the winter and cool in
the summer. The women also burn cow dung inside the hut
to keep mosquitoes away.

Vanilla Poop

Japanese scientists have found a new way to make
vanilla ice cream. They use cow poop! The scientists
use the poop to make vanillin. Vanillin gives vanilla its
flavor. The scientists make the vanillin by heating and
applying a lot of pressure to the poop. The heat kills
any bacteria in the dung.

You can't buy cow-dung ice cream in stores.
Scientists think people would be too grossed out.
Instead, the vanillin can be used in candles, shampoo,
and other products.

dung—solid waste from animals

Chapter 2

AROUND TOWN

Sewer plants. Garbage dumps.
Every town has its own revolting places.

Work Out

People go to gyms to stay healthy. They lift weights and do other types of exercise to get strong and lose weight.

But people aren't the only things that hang out at gyms. Germs are getting a workout too! People sweat when they use exercise machines. Sweat carries germs. When people get off the machines, they leave germs behind.

Dumbbells and bike seats are among the dirtiest places in a gym. Many people don't wipe off dumbbells or seats when they are finished, so germs are left for the next person to pick up. People also carry germs into gyms on their sneakers.

What's the filthiest place of all? The answer may surprise you. It's the shower! Showers are wet. Showers are warm. Showers are the perfect place for germs to live. Athlete's foot is an infection caused by a fungus that a person can get from a gym shower.

But there are ways to protect yourself from gym germs. Use antibacterial wipes to clean the exercise machines and weights you touch. Sit on a clean towel rather than right on the seats of machines. Wearing flip-flops in the shower can help too.

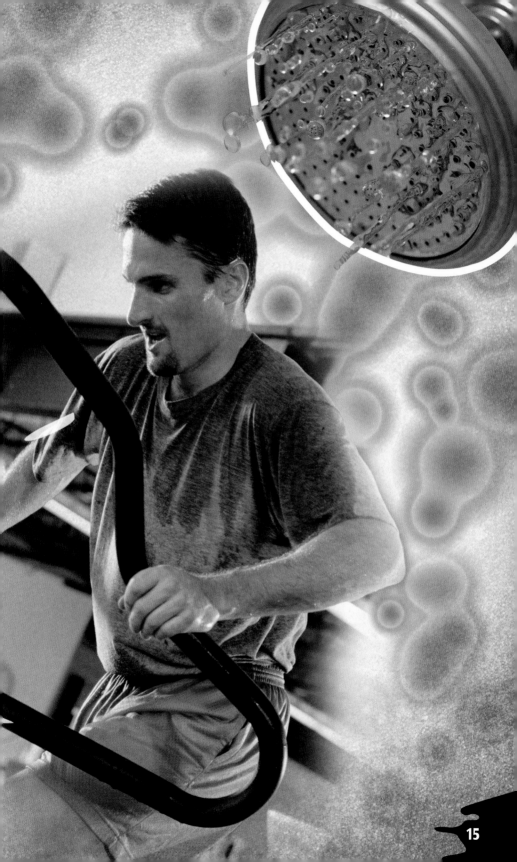

A Stinky Journey

What happens to poop after you flush? It takes a trip to the sewer plant.

All you have to do is pull the handle. After you flush, the dirty water travels through pipes. Those pipes connect to a sewer system. At the end of the line is a sewer plant. Sewer plants clean the bacteria out of the toilet water.

People flush many things down the toilet that are not meant to be flushed. Rags. Sticks. Diapers. A dead goldfish or two. The sewer plant's first job is to remove these objects. Then the plant really begins working. It kills harmful bacteria in the water. How? Inside the sewer plants are large pools of poop and wastewater. Plant workers put bacteria in the pools. The bacteria eat the organic matter in the wastewater.

What the bacteria can't eat sinks to the bottom of the pool. The water on top is now clean. It can go back into the environment. The sludge at the bottom is scooped up. In the past, the sludge was usually buried. Now, it is often burned in a big furnace that generates electricity.

 organic—produced by animals or plants

Smelly Fuel

Scientists have learned how to make energy from poop. They mix human waste with oxygen-hungry microbes. These tiny creatures break down the waste and create methane gas. The gas can be burned to heat a house or make electricity.

The solid waste is first separated from the liquid waste at sewer plants.

microbe—a tiny living thing that is too small to be seen without a microscope

A Heap of Trash

Americans throw away 243 million tons
(220 million metric tons) of trash each year.
Where does it all go?

Rotting food. Dirty diapers. Bags of used cat litter. Soiled tissues.
Dirty rags. Chicken bones. Most of our garbage ends up in landfills.
Landfills are where workers bury garbage under layers of dirt.

Landfills smell like, well, garbage. In a landfill, meat rots. So do
vegetables and fruit. The rotting food releases a gas called methane.

Landfills are crawling with rats. Rats don't seem to mind the smell.
They eat rotten food before it is buried. A landfill is also like a
cafeteria for flies. Flies land on rotting food. They vomit on the food to
make it easier to eat.

When the flies finish eating, they lay eggs on the rotting food. The eggs
hatch, and maggots crawl out. These worm-like critters eat the food and
grow into adult flies.

Cockroaches find plenty to eat at landfills too. One of the things they
eat is the glue found on envelopes, stamps, and boxes. Hundreds of
thousands of the pests can live in a landfill.

Nasty
Neighborhood

Niagara Falls is a natural wonder. Nearby Love Canal is not.

William T. Love wanted to build homes near Niagara Falls, New York. In the early 1900s, he dug a canal to move water. He wanted to use the water to generate electricity, but his plan cost too much money. Love gave up on the project.

The empty canal sat for years. In the 1920s, a company started using the canal to bury chemicals. In the late 1950s, 100 homes were built near the canal. People began living in the homes. They named the area Love Canal.

In the 1970s, tubs of unsafe chemicals broke through the ground. More than 80 different chemicals were found at Love Canal. Trees and gardens turned black and died. When people living in the area began to get sick, they blamed the chemicals.

People left their homes and did not return. It took 21 years to clean up the mess. There are still a lot of chemicals buried underground. No one lives at Love Canal today.

pollution from a factory in Russia

DANGER
CHEMICAL
WASTE
SITE
KEEP OUT

Chapter 3

NAUSEATING NATURE

With green trees and colorful flowers, nature is often beautiful. Look a little deeper and you will find that nature can also be revolting.

Poopy Cave

When Mexican free-tailed bats want to go on vacation, they stay at a cave filled with poop!

Every spring, 20 million bats **migrate** 1,000 miles (1,609 kilometers) to Bracken Cave in Texas. The bats travel there from their winter home in Mexico to raise their young. A single bat might eat 3,000 insects each night. All those bugs mean a whole lot of bat poop, or guano, in the cave. How much? In some places it's 70 feet (21 meters) deep!

The cave's floor is covered in guano. Bacteria and fungi eat the guano. But there are so many bats that the guano piles up faster than the bacteria and fungi can eat it.

migrate—to move from one place to another when seasons change or to find food

23

Revolting River

About 20 years ago, the Citarum River in Indonesia was beautiful. Birds flocked to its shores. Villagers used its water to grow rice.

But today, the Citarum River is an open sewer. It is choked with the human waste and trash of millions of people. People pick through the rubbish for things they can sell. Most of the fish have died and there is very little life in the river.

Why is the river so dirty? Dozens of factories started dumping chemicals into the water. Those chemicals killed plants and fish. People also began to pour human waste into the river because there is not a good sewer system in Indonesia.

Still, villagers have no choice but to water their gardens with the filthy water. Some people drink from the river. People boil the water to kill germs before they drink it. But boiling does not get rid of poisons from the chemicals.

Other Dirty Rivers

The Citarum is only one of many filthy rivers. Here are other rivers that are among the world's dirtiest:

- Ganges River (India)
- Yangtze River (China)
- Pripyat River (Eastern Europe)
- Yellow River (China)
- Matanza-Riachuelo River (Argentina)

Toxic Lake

Fifty years ago, there were many fish and shrimp in China's Lake Tai. Farmers used the lake to water their crops. Today the lake is a polluted mess!

Toxic pollutants have turned the lake an eerie green. Two million people live near the water's edge. They can no longer drink or cook with the water. They also can't fish in the lake or water their crops from it.

Why is the lake so filthy? Chemical factories dump waste into the lake. The waste pollutes the lake. It also destroys the oxygen that fish need, causing the fish to die. The chemicals kill the lake's plants too.

FACT

Nearly two out of every 10 rivers and lakes in China are so polluted that many farmers can no longer use the water to grow crops.

toxic—poisonous

Chapter 4

FILTHY FARMS

Old MacDonald had a farm, but it sure wasn't as disgusting as these filthy farms.

Horrid Hog Farms

Bacon goes great with eggs. Where that bacon comes from might turn your stomach.

Most hogs in the United States live on big hog farms. Hogs are stuffed into buildings as long as football fields. The animals live in tiny crates. There is little room for the hogs to move. All they do is eat and **defecate**. When they are big enough, the hogs become food.

North Carolina has close to 10 million hogs. There are more hogs in North Carolina than people. All those hogs produce 19 million tons (17 million metric tons) of waste a year. That's a lot of poop!

The waste sits in huge pits. These pits release a smelly, toxic gas called hydrogen sulfide. The gas has made some people who live near the farms ill. In 1995 a pit burst at a hog farm in North Carolina. Twenty-five million gallons (95 million liters) of hog waste poured into a river. Disgusting!

hog barn

defecate—to expel feces

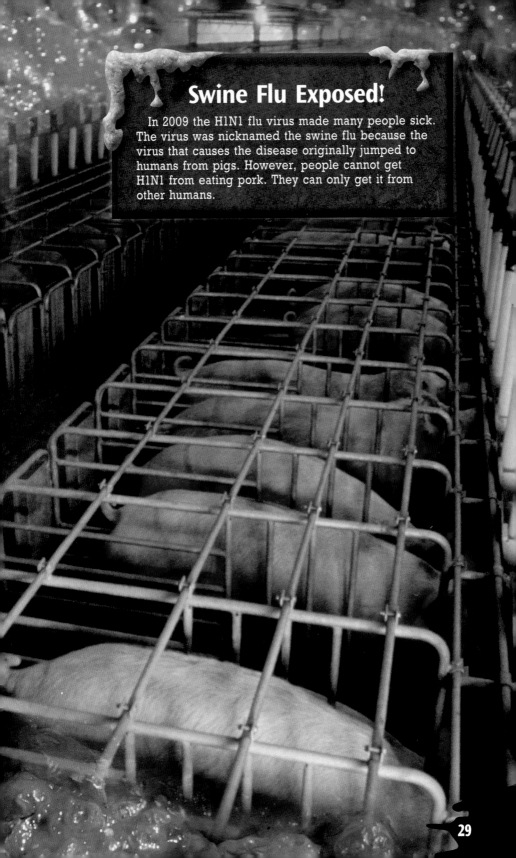

Swine Flu Exposed!

In 2009 the H1N1 flu virus made many people sick. The virus was nicknamed the swine flu because the virus that causes the disease originally jumped to humans from pigs. However, people cannot get H1N1 from eating pork. They can only get it from other humans.

Putrid Poultry Farms

Why did the chicken cross the road?
To get out of the poultry farm, of course.

Jokes about chickens might make us laugh, but poultry farming is not a joke. Around 8 billion chickens die each year in the United States when they become food for humans. Most spend their lives in very crowded indoor chicken farms. The buildings are so crowded that chickens often walk over one another to get to their food.

Some animals are packed in cages. Farmers trim the animals' beaks and toes. They want to keep the birds from hurting themselves and each other. The animals are fed a special diet so they grow very big, very quickly. This practice causes many chickens to die. Their bodies cannot handle the strain.

Egg-laying hens live in cages on top of one another. Poop from one cage falls onto the chickens below. Heaps of chicken waste make poultry farms smell bad.

Chicken farms pollute the environment too. In 1997 the waste from a chicken farm in Maryland poured into a river. Millions of fish died. People got rashes from touching the water.

FACT

Thirty thousand egg-laying
hens can produce 40 tons
(36 metric tons) of manure
a month. That's 480 tons
(435 metric tons) of chicken
poop a year!

Weird Worm Farms

Fishermen need worms. So do farmers and gardeners.

A worm farm is a one-stop grocery store for worm products. Worm farming is called vermiculture. Farmers raise worms for their poop because it is rich in **nutrients**. Worm poop is sold to gardeners to use as plant food. Gardeners soak bags of worm poop in water. They pour the poop on their vegetable plants. The mixture helps plants grow.

nutrient—a substance needed by a living thing to stay healthy

Worms are raised in bins of soil. Farmers put in scraps of fruit, vegetables, and bread for food. They pour water into the bins to keep the dirt moist. Every worm bin also has good and bad bacteria growing in it.

It is not a good sign if a worm farm smells. It means bacteria are growing. It also means there is too much food for the worms to gobble up. Instead, the bacteria eat the food. The food rots quickly and smells awful.

If there is too little oxygen, the bad bacteria kill the good bacteria and make the water, also known as leachate, toxic. This toxic water can make people sick. Many worm farms have wastewater treatment systems that process the water and other wastes and turn them into fertilizer.

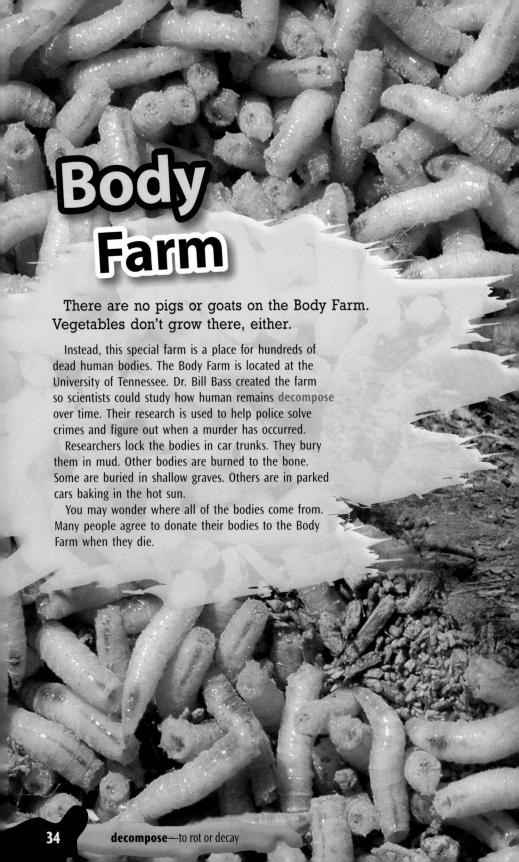

Body Farm

There are no pigs or goats on the Body Farm.
Vegetables don't grow there, either.

Instead, this special farm is a place for hundreds of
dead human bodies. The Body Farm is located at the
University of Tennessee. Dr. Bill Bass created the farm
so scientists could study how human remains decompose
over time. Their research is used to help police solve
crimes and figure out when a murder has occurred.

Researchers lock the bodies in car trunks. They bury
them in mud. Other bodies are burned to the bone.
Some are buried in shallow graves. Others are in parked
cars baking in the hot sun.

You may wonder where all of the bodies come from.
Many people agree to donate their bodies to the Body
Farm when they die.

decompose—to rot or decay

Flesh on the Menu

Scientists can tell how long a body has been rotting by studying the different types of bugs that feed on it.

Flies are the first to land on a corpse. The flies eat the rotting tissue. Then they lay eggs in the body's mouth and ears. Soon, maggots appear. Maggots feast on rotting flesh. The body's temperature rises as more maggots feast. When there is no more flesh to eat, the body begins to dry out. When that happens, other bugs arrive to feed on the maggots.

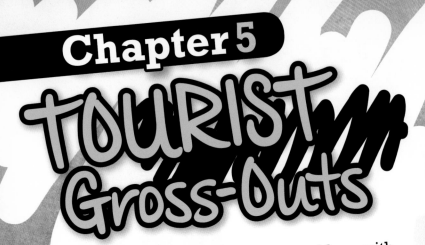

Chapter 5

TOURIST Gross-Outs

You might want to pack a barf bag with your toothbrush if you ever go on vacation to one of these tourist sites.

Pushy Pigeons

St. Mark's Square in Venice, Italy, is old and beautiful. Thousands of tourists visit this site each year. But one ugly sight might take tourists by surprise!

It is an old tradition for tourists to feed birdseed to pigeons in St. Mark's Square. Each day thousands of pigeons gather there for the food. The pushy birds have ruffled a few feathers. Many people have begun calling them pests. Some even call them "rats with wings." The pigeons claw and peck at the statues in the square.

Usually pigeons don't eat and sleep in the same place. But with so many tourists providing food, about 130,000 pigeons have changed their habits. They now live permanently in the square. They make nests on building ledges or even on statues. All of these birds make a lot of pigeon poop.

Pigeon guano is like acid. It damages buildings and marble statues. It gets all over tables, chairs, and benches in the square. It even lands in people's hair! For years, people have tried to get rid of the birds, but not much has worked.

In 2008 the city passed a law banning the sale of birdseed. But the birds still come to feed. They find bread crumbs and other things to eat.

Temple of Rats

Rats have a bad reputation. They carry disease. They chew through wood. But in one place at least, rats are adored.

That place is called the Karni Mata Temple. The temple is in India. It was built by Hindus to honor the rat goddess Karni Mata. Hindus believe the souls of the goddess' followers live inside the rats. The temple has beautiful marble floors. It is decorated in silver and gold. It's also filled with rats! There are about 20,000 rats living in the temple.

The temple's priests protect the rats from hungry birds. The rats run over visitors' feet. They even join people during meals. The rats drink huge bowls of milk. They chow down on grain and sweets. Thousands of Hindus travel to see the rats each year.

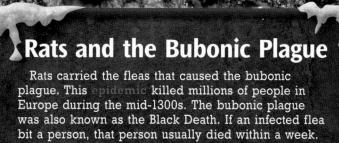

Rats and the Bubonic Plague

Rats carried the fleas that caused the bubonic plague. This epidemic killed millions of people in Europe during the mid-1300s. The bubonic plague was also known as the Black Death. If an infected flea bit a person, that person usually died within a week.

Today wild rodents can still carry the diseased fleas. About 10 to 15 people in the United States become infected with the plague each year. Doctors treat the disease with antibiotics.

epidemic—an infectious disease that affects a large number of people at the same time
antibiotic—a drug that kills bacteria and is used to cure infections and disease

Bubble Gum Alley

What do you do with your chewed gum?
Swallow it? Wrap it in paper and throw it away?

In San Luis Obispo, California, people stick their gum on a 50-foot (15-meter) long wall in an alley. For years people have been sticking wads of gum there. Eventually, the alley became known as Bubble Gum Alley.

No one knows when the chewy tradition began. Some say it started in the 1940s. Others say the 1950s.

No matter. By the 1970s, the walls of the alley were covered in used gum. Shop owners were disgusted. They said the wall was dirty and unhealthy. But people continued to stick their gum there. Now it is a popular tourist site. The city encourages people to visit, chew a piece of gum, and stick it on the wall.

But think twice before you visit. The alley smells like mold and the sidewalk in the alley is littered with hard gum.

Bubble Gum Alley

Seattle Gum Wall

Seattle, Washington, has its own sticky tourist site. The Wall of Gum is about 50 feet (15 meters) long. The owners of the wall had it cleaned several times. They gave up in 1998. That's when tourists started coming to see the gummy wall.

How much gum is on the wall? No one knows. But it's several inches thick in some places.

Cockroach
Hall of Fame

People say that the dog is man's best friend. But there is one man who prefers cockroaches.

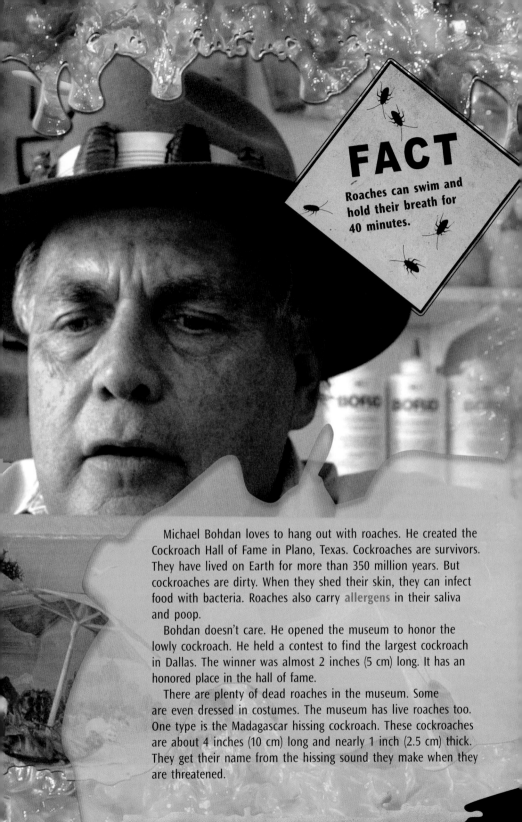

FACT

Roaches can swim and hold their breath for 40 minutes.

Michael Bohdan loves to hang out with roaches. He created the Cockroach Hall of Fame in Plano, Texas. Cockroaches are survivors. They have lived on Earth for more than 350 million years. But cockroaches are dirty. When they shed their skin, they can infect food with bacteria. Roaches also carry allergens in their saliva and poop.

Bohdan doesn't care. He opened the museum to honor the lowly cockroach. He held a contest to find the largest cockroach in Dallas. The winner was almost 2 inches (5 cm) long. It has an honored place in the hall of fame.

There are plenty of dead roaches in the museum. Some are even dressed in costumes. The museum has live roaches too. One type is the Madagascar hissing cockroach. These cockroaches are about 4 inches (10 cm) long and nearly 1 inch (2.5 cm) thick. They get their name from the hissing sound they make when they are threatened.

allergen—something that makes a person have an allergic reaction

Mütter Museum

Brains, skeletons, and shrunken heads. Welcome to the Mütter Museum!

Located in Philadelphia, Pennsylvania, the Mütter Museum is a medical creep show. It's packed with more than 20,000 bizarre objects.

One is a tumor from the mouth of former U.S. President Grover Cleveland. The tumor is the size of a golf ball. It floats in a small jar. The museum is also home to the "Soap Lady." The fat in her body turned into a soap-like material. Scientists are trying to find out why that happened, as well as when and how she died.

Another sight to see at the museum is the liver of Chang and Eng Bunker. They were once the world's most famous conjoined twins. They were part of P. T. Barnum's circus troupe in the early 1800s. Barnum heavily advertised the twins, and many people came to the circus to see them.

The museum also has a small piece of bone from John Wilkes Booth. Booth was the actor who killed former U.S. President Abraham Lincoln.

One of the most interesting things at the Mütter Museum is the shrunken head collection. The heads come from a tribe of warriors who lived in Ecuador and Peru. These warriors cut off the heads of their enemies. They then shrunk the heads by boiling them in pots of simmering water. They believed that shrinking the heads kept the souls from escaping from the heads.

conjoined—joined together

The museum has a plaster cast of the bodies of Chan and Eng Bunker.

A Place for Everyone

Here's hoping you enjoyed the journey through these horrible places. Which location was the most revolting? What's the most disgusting place you can think of?

Glossary

allergen (A-luhr-jen)—something that makes a person have an allergic reaction

antibiotic (an-ti-bye-OT-ik)—a drug that kills bacteria and is used to cure infections and disease

bacteria (bak-TEER-ee-uh)—very small living things that exist all around you and inside you; some bacteria cause disease

conjoined (kon-JOIND)—joined together

decompose (dee-kuhm-POHZ)—to rot or decay

defecate (DEF-i-kate)—to expel feces

dung (DUHNG)—solid waste from animals

epidemic (ep-i-DEM-ik)—an infectious disease that affects a large number of people at the same time

humidity (hyoo-MIH-du-tee)—the measure of the moisture in the air

immune system (i-MYOON SISS-tuhm)—the part of the body that protects against germs and diseases

microbe (MYE-krobe)—a tiny living thing that is too small to be seen without a microscope

migrate (MYE-grate)—to move from one place to another when seasons change or to find food

musty (MUHS-tee)—smelly, old, or damp

nutrient (NOO-tree-uhnt)—a substance needed by a living thing to stay healthy

organic (or-GAN-ik)—produced by animals or plants

spore (SPOR)—a plant cell that develops into a new plant

toxic (TOK-sik)—poisonous

Read More

Claybourne, Anna. *100 Most Disgusting Things on the Planet and What to Do to Avoid Them.* New York: Scholastic, 2010.

Corrick, James. *Gritty, Stinky Ancient Egypt: The Disgusting Details about Life in Ancient Egypt.* Disgusting History. Mankato, Minn.: Capstone Press, 2011.

Platt, Richard. *Plagues, Pox, and Pestilence.* New York: Kingfisher, 2011.

Internet Sites

FactHound offers a safe, fun way to find Internet sites related to this book. All of the sites on FactHound have been researched by our staff.

Here's all you do:

Visit *www.facthound.com*

Type in this code: **9781429675338**

Index